W9-AOW-050

THE POWER OF ENOUGH
Finding Contentment
By Putting Stuff In It's Place

By Lynn A. Miller

MMA, 2003
Printed by Evangel Press
Nappanee, Indiana

The Power of Enough
Finding Contentment by Putting Stuff in Its Place
Copyright © 2003 Lynn A. Miller

Unless otherwise noted, Scripture taken from New American Standard version.

Cover Design by: Karen S. Schmucker

Library of Congress Cataloging-in-Publication Data 2003112953

Printed in the United States of America.
10 9 8 7 6 5 4 3 2 1 / 12 11 10 09 08 07 06 05 04 03

Table of contents

Introduction:

While living in Chicago in 1998, I signed up to take a graduate school course called Investment Management and Portfolio Analysis—just for the fun of it. The course was offered by the Xavier University business school, but the classes met above the Mercantile Exchange on Wacker Boulevard in downtown Chicago. The course was fun—at least for me and the one other fellow in the class who was taking it "just for fun." He'd just sold a home health-care company he and his wife had started ten years earlier, and they were sitting on four million dollars they didn't know what to do with.

I was working in a voluntary service assignment with a local church on the west side of Chicago, living in the neighborhood and making $64 a month plus room and board. We couldn't have been from more different sides of the economic fence. But both of us were taking the course just because we wanted to know more about how the world of finance works. And we both got A's in the course!

The other students were either commodity traders or bond traders who needed to take the course if they ever hoped to escape the high pressure world of the trading floor. They had to take it to survive in the financial marketplace. I don't know what kind of grades the rest of the class got, but I do know that the others didn't enjoy the experience nearly as much my friend and I did.

The most valuable thing I learned from that course was not how to determine the inherent value of a stock by using the "discount dividend formula" or how to find the "efficient frontier" for a particular portfolio. The most valuable thing was realizing that how you approach something depends a great deal on the reason you're doing it. I was taking the course because I wanted to learn something; most of the other students were taking it because they had to learn something. My want to reason for taking the course was what made all the difference. It gave me the power to do well.

And that's why I've written this book. About halfway through my first ten years of traveling from church to church trying to explain the first book I wrote about stewardship, Firstfruits Living, I committed myself to not writing any more books! I like to travel, but it's tough to keep a marriage going when you're gone three or four days a week for nine months a year and only able to go to church with your wife six or eight Sundays a year.

However, I want people to understand my message, so for some time I've been trying to figure out what was wrong with the first book that made it difficult for people to get the point just by reading it. A couple years ago I discovered that something was missing from Firstfruits Living. What was missing was essential for understanding that God has a plan to "give us away" and that stewardship is the act of organizing your life to make that possible.

The missing ingredient was contentment, the power behind good stewardship. Plenty of books out there proclaim other good reasons to want to be a good steward of your life, reasons like profit, obedience, or even worship. Most of those are good reasons indeed. But none of them have the power to make it happen. None that is, except contentment. Contentment gives one the ability to know when "enough is enough." That's where the power comes from. Consider the following example.

I've discovered that I love getting phone calls from telemarketers. Maybe I shouldn't love it so much, but I get a real kick out of listening to their sales pitches telling me why I should buy their product that's guaranteed to make my life so much more satisfying. Some time ago I got a call from someone in Florida trying to sell me a septic tank additive. This lady went on and on about the necessity of having the right amount of the right kind of bacteria in my septic tank to avoid having problems with bad drainage and blocked pipes. She described the awful task of digging up a drain field to replace the clogged tile, and the horrible smell from the messy pools of "black water" that indicated you had a plugged system. She also detailed the high cost of fixing all that, and how for just a fraction of that cost—by buying her product and using it regularly—I could avoid all that expense and difficulty.

Fortunately, when I'd had a new septic system put in, the county engineer had sent me some material on how a septic system works. I was prepared for this kind of sales pitch. But instead of arguing with the lady about the necessity of putting more bacteria in a system that gets bacteria naturally when you use the system, I just said to her, "Thank you very much for your concern, but I have enough bacteria in my system and more bacteria will not make me happier." And without even saying a word, she hung up! Now if you can get a tele-marketer to hang up on you, that is power!

More bacteria in my septic system wouldn't make me happier, and more things in my life won't make me happier either. That's contentment. For it to really make a difference in your life, you can't just say the words; you have to feel what they mean. My task in this book is to help you understand where contentment comes from. My prayer is that as you read you will not only discover what "stuff" means to you, but that you'll also experience the power of putting stuff in its place. That's where contentment comes from: putting stuff in the role that God gave it, and not letting it mean something God doesn't intend it to mean. Stuff, after all, was created by God. And everything created by God is good! Stuff is good, but it has its place.

Chapter One

The Pursuit of Happiness

What makes us happy? That's easy: a close, loving family; a warm, safe home; a good, solid relationship with God. Simple, right? Well, at least those are the things that are supposed to make us happy. If you go to church you know that those certainly are the right answers to the question. But even in the church those answers don't seem to represent what's actually happening. For if you see how people actually live when they're not in church, you'll find that some of them are seeking happiness elsewhere, primarily in consumption.

Now consumption itself isn't necessarily a problem. In fact, not consuming air means you'll die pretty quickly. Likewise, consuming food and water is an essential activity for survival. But somewhere in the history of humankind consumption stopped being purely a matter of survival and started being a focus of happiness.

Shopping has become a major source of entertainment in Western societies, and the accumulation of stuff has become the road to happiness. As a result, personal bankruptcies are at an all-time high, as are credit card carry-over balances. Personal savings are at one of the lowest rates in the industrialized world. And rental storage facilities are springing up everywhere, even in suburbia where the average home square-footage is the largest in the world. If happiness comes with simplicity, there must be a lot of unhappy people out there.

No matter where you go in the world, people are in love with stuff. Bumper-stickers proclaim, "He who dies with the most toys wins." Or," My other car is a boat." And the most shameless consumption statement of all is the bumper sticker on the monster motor home headed for Florida that brags, "We're spending our children's inheritance."

The most successful e-commerce startup in the entire world is eBay, the online auction site where an enormous amount of "stuff" is bought and sold each minute. And it isn't just useful stuff that's traded, it is also advertising about stuff. In the summer of 2002 I finished building a sailboat that I'd been working on for eight long years. I needed to find a used outboard motor to get the boat in and out of harbors. So I went online to the eBay web site. First I selected Sports Equipment from the list of categories, then Boats and Motors, then Motors. And then I had to sort through hundreds of items that were not motors at all. People were selling posters and fliers that described motors sold fifty and sixty years ago. Some people actually collect antique advertising, not really useable stuff but the stuff that was used to sell stuff back then. Stuff you might call "old stuff about old stuff"!

The production and sale of stuff is the way companies achieve what the world of business is all about: getting my money into their pockets. Once you get beneath all the fluff about the "nation-building benefits" of globalization (increased employment, new infrastructure, etc), it all boils down to a competitive search for the cheapest labor. After all, the less a company has to spend on producing stuff to sell to me, the more of my money it can keep in its pocket. That money is the "earnings" of a corporation. And good earnings reports drive the value of a company (and its stock price) up. That means that stockholders and executives make more money so they can buy more stuff from other companies that make stuff so that the stockholders and executives can have happier lives!

The accumulation of stuff to achieve happiness is what living the American Dream is all about. We even have it codified in our Bill of Rights: "Life, Liberty, And the Pursuit of Happiness."

There's nothing wrong with being happy, but the world of advertising is getting better and better at telling us that happiness is found in accumulating stuff: "Drive this car, wear these clothes, invest with us, vacation here, and you'll be happy." Pictures of smiling, happy, beautiful people walking barefoot on sandy beaches sell everything from airline tickets to investment advice. The happiness of laughing, gray-haired seniors is ascribed to everything from laxatives to liquid food supplements to driving the latest four-wheel drive SUV down a paved road.

The problem is that the American dream has turned into a financial nightmare for a lot of people who feel helpless in the face of the onslaught coming from Madison Avenue. Why is that? What is it that makes us so susceptible to the proposition that "more" will make us happier? Is it happiness that's really being sold here? Or is it something deeper within us that we hope buying stuff will satisfy?

A surprising statistic got me wondering about this

question. It's recently been reported that Prozac (the anti-depressant "happiness" pill) is not the most widely prescribed "psycho-pharmaceutical" drug. Instead, it's Xanax, an anti-anxiety drug. What we seek is not so much a state of giggling happiness, but a relief from the nagging anxiety that plagues our everyday lives. Lowered anxiety is the Holy Grail of the pursuit of happiness. And the mother of all anxiety is the question, "Who am I"?

Which leads us back to stuff. Remember the car ads? If you listen carefully to the message that's projected you'll hear not only that this car will make you happy, but that this car will make you somebody. This car will wipe out the anxiety that comes from the nagging thought that maybe you really aren't anybody after all.

The world of advertising tells us that the answer to the existential question of the ages, "Why am I here?" is finally here! We are here, the TV tells us, to be consumers: to buy and accumulate and store and buy more. We are here to be consumers because consuming will make us happy! The problem is, it isn't working. We're not happy. North American society as a whole not only is not happy, but the U.S. part of it is very anxious. Fear is the number one emotional state in the world today; ironically that is especially so in the only superpower left in the world.

On a recent National Public Radio All Things Considered radio news show, I heard five news reports in a row that detailed what we're afraid of. The first story was about Californians paying $1300 for a full-body MRI scan simply because they're afraid that something might be going wrong somewhere in their bodies. Then there was a report about the fear that North Korea created by turning off the surveillance cameras in their single nuclear reactor. Following that was a story about the search for Al Qaeda leaders and the fear that they're planning another major terrorist strike. Then I heard something about the problems of deciding who to vaccinate for smallpox just in case our fears about bio-terrorism are realized. And finally the news reported on the speech by President George W. Bush justifying a pre-emptive strike on Baghdad because of his fear that Saddam Hussein would use weapons of mass-destruction against the U.S.

Five fears in a row, and ironically, the answer to all of them related to stuff: vaccines, bombs, searches, MRIs, cameras, etc. If stuff brings happiness, then something is wrong because happiness is in short supply no matter where you live. In the U.S. we have more stuff than anyone in the world at any time in history, but we still are not happy.

Study Questions

1. What does "happy" feel like to you? Can you describe the sensation of being happy? Is it a feeling of excited joy or of quiet satisfaction?

2. What makes you happy? When do you feel what happiness means to you? Is it when you begin a new project or when a chore is finished to your satisfaction? Is it when you're in the presence of someone you love? Is it the fun of shopping or the delight of getting something you want on sale?

3. Is there a "thing" in your possession that makes you happy? Does wearing a particular piece of clothing bring that feeling that you described in your answer to question one?

4. Do you have something that you bought that you thought would make you happy that no longer does?

5. Can you describe who you are in one sentence?

2

Chapter Two

Where Happiness Comes From

My favorite movie quote of all time comes from my all-time favorite movie, Out of Africa, starring Meryll Streep and Robert Redford. It's a true story of how a woman named Karen Blixen left Europe and went to Africa to build a farm out of the bush in colonial Kenya. For some reason, I really identify with that movie. I don't know if it's the gorgeous scenery that sweeps me away, or the fact that I also built a farm out of the bush in rural Botswana in the late 1970s.

Right in the middle of the movie, one particular line both changed my life and had a part in the creation of this book. Baroness von has gone home to Denmark to recover from a disease. As she returns, she is met at her home by all the workers on the farm. Farad, the Muslim servant in charge of her house, is standing at the open doorway. Farad is a dignified Somali, in his own mind far above the local Kikuyu tribes-people—and the British colonialists for that matter. But he is devoted to Baroness Blixen and would do anything for her. He knows her as a woman of courage and strength, and he knows of her love for Africa and its people.

When Baroness Blixen approaches the house, she sees Farad and greets him. She asks him, "Are you well, Farad?" Farad replies, "I am well enough, Msabu."

Now that is good theology! Especially good stewardship theology. But it's not very common theology, especially in our society. "I am well enough" is a statement of contentment that goes against the entire American cultural value system.

Think about it. Have you ever heard anything advertised that claims that it is "good enough"? Who would buy something that was just good enough? Good enough motor oil? Good enough breakfast cereal? The only thing I can think of close to that is Ralph's Pretty Good Grocery in Lake Woebegon. But that's a mythical store in a mythical town in a radio show, all a fiction from Garrison Keillor's imagination. And anyway, it's "pretty good" rather than just good enough. What is it that makes something good enough so unthinkable in our world?

Paul's letter to the Philippians is a personal letter from both Paul and Timothy to a church they've visited and know well. At the end of the letter, Paul thanks the congregation for their concern for him personally and for a gift that they sent to him. But in his thanks to them Paul also tells them that he was not as desperate as he might have seemed to be, for he has learned to be content in what ever circumstances he finds himself in.

"Not that I speak from want, for I have learned to be content in whatever circumstances I am. I know how to get along with humble means, and I also know how to live in prosperity; in any and every circumstance I have learned the secret of being filled and going hungry, both of having abundance and suffering need" (Philippians 4:11-12).

I want to point out two quick things from this text. First, contentment is something that must be learned. Contentment is not inherited, not automatically a part of your emotional repertoire. At best it's something that we need to relearn. We may have been born knowing when enough is enough—at least as it relates to food. After all, babies tend to stop eating when they're full. Adults, on the other hand—especially American adults—tend to stop eating only when they're stuffed.

Maybe that's because we've all grown up with mothers who believe that if their children don't eat a full plate of a balanced diet at every meal, they'll have been proven to be horribly bad mothers. Most mothers figure out by the third or forth child that if the kid has enough strength to push the chair away from the table and actually get up and walk away, he probably has had enough to eat, at least for the time being. But still, "finish your plate" is probably the most common thing ever said to any child at dinner time. And we all know what comes next, don't we? "There are children starving in _____!" In 1944 when I first heard those words, it was Europe.

No matter how it begins, the desire for more seems to be present in everyone in one form or another. And the world of consumer advertising knows that all too well. "More is better!" is the message that comes from Madison Avenue. Bigger cars, bigger boxes of laundry detergent, more free airline miles, higher interest, more of everything. The missing value in all those ads is "enough." After all, how much more can you sell to people who know they have enough?

The second thing I want to glean from Philippians 4:11-12 is a clue about the key to contentment. Paul says it's a secret. That means that it's not readily apparent to the casual observer. And you can be sure that no one in the commercial world is going to tell you what it is. After all, with this secret you can resist every Madison Avenue technique ever invented.

The secret itself is in the very next verse, Philippians 4:13: "I can do all things through him who strengthens me." "Oh, no," someone is thinking right now, "not another metaphysical 'turn it over to Jesus' trick." You remember that kind of simplistic answer, "let go and let God."

No, this isn't a sleight-of-hand trick or wishful thinking. This is simply a realization that our relationship with Christ is what gives us strength, and not the stuff we have. We've been convinced somewhere along the way that we're weak without more stuff, and that's the problem.

Think about the language we use. A financially strong company is one that has more money than a financially weak company. A strong man has more muscles than a weak man. A strong cup of coffee has more caffeine than a weak cup of coffee. A strong battery has more juice than a weak battery. You get the point. More equals strength. But Paul says that the secret of contentment is learning to be strengthened not by prosperity or being filled, but through Christ.

The reason we find it so hard to be content is that we've been trying all our lives to be strong people by accumulating stuff. The problem is that there's absolutely no evidence that it works. In fact, the evidence says that it doesn't work. Does wealth equal strength? Well, maybe it provides the kind of strength that allows one to fulfill one's every whim. But certainly not the strength that gives one the power to avoid buying everything one can afford, and then some.

Some of the weakest people right now in terms of emotional stability and anxiety about the future are people who did really well in the "bull market" of the 90s. For many of these people, money meant security, and when the bubble burst so did their security. The sad thing is that although many of them still have far more money than they'll ever need, their lives have become focused on protecting what they've not lost.

Money can mean security, at least in North American society. If you don't have enough food to feed your family, finding food becomes the focus of your life. If you're home-less because of a job loss or natural disaster, finding shelter will be your focus until you achieve it. And money can solve both of those needs. But once you have enough, more money becomes a burden, not greater security. It's an inter-esting paradox: too little creates insecurity, and too much also creates insecurity.

It's a little like a see-saw with a big box of money on one end. If the box is on the "too little end" of the plank, you're stuck in "insecurity" not knowing where your next meal or the rent is coming from.

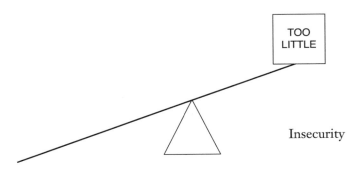

If you have too much money it's like a see-saw with the box of money on the other end; you're stuck in the insecuri-ty while you worry about protecting your excess from infla-tion and market fluctuation.

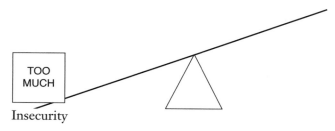

Insecurity

But if you have "enough" money—not too little and not too much—then the see-saw zone is balanced in security.

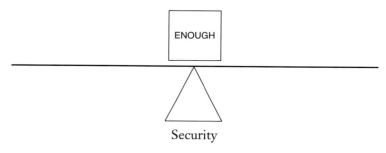

Security

In 2 Corinthians 8 and 9, Paul is raising money to help meet a need in the church at Jerusalem. And in 2 Corinthians 8:13-15 he assures the Corinthian believers that this offering is not for the ease of the members in Jerusalem, nor that the Corinthians would be afflicted. He tells them that their abundance is a supply for someone else's needs, and that it works the other way as well: someone else's abundance will be a supply for their need. And then he quotes Exodus16:18 for his reasoning: "As it is written, 'He who gathered much did not have too much, and he who gathered little had no lack'." The Biblical mandate is clear. God intends that everyone have enough—not too little and not too much.

That's the good news! There's enough for everyone! But when someone has too much, someone else will not have enough. That was especially true in pre-modern times. In that "subsistence" economy, if one person was wealthy then a lot of people had to be poor. But modern economists tell us that we now live in a surplus economy. There is enough for everyone, and in some cases too much. When there is too much, then prices fall in response to the lack of demand. The problem is, even those who have enough want more. And that "more" too often comes from those who already have little.

Several years ago I traveled to the city of San Salvador in Central America. There I met a family who was paying twice what they had been paying for electricity only three years earlier. When I asked why, they told me that the government of El Salvador had previously owned the electric company. But under pressure from the International Monetary Fund and the U.S. Department of the Treasury, the company was sold to a private U.S. energy corporation. Immediately the price of electricity went up 20%, and after only three years people were paying double what they had before. The price increases were due to the demand for higher profits by the management and shareholders of the new company. Those who were already wealthy enough to be investors were not satisfied with their wealth and wanted more! And it had to come from the pockets of people who already were having trouble finding enough. The Salvadoran people resented becoming poorer so that someone else could become richer.

No wonder having too much does not bring security or peace; your abundance belongs to someone else—those who have needs. Paul's understanding of the role of stuff is the updated version of Malachi's charge to the Israelites in Malachi 3: "Will a man rob God? Yet you are robbing me!" The Israelites were holding back some of the tithe and were robbing God. When we accumulate beyond what we need, we too are robbing someone: anyone on God's earth who doesn't have enough. It's scary to think that having more than you need is the same as robbing someone. If not God, then God's people.

Study Questions

1. What do you buy that you shop for in terms of it being "good enough"? Is there such a thing as a good enough laundry soap or a good enough food item?

2. In what areas of your life do you feel particularly strong? Do you feel that you're strong in your educational level? Are you in a position of strength financially?

3. Go through your closet and look at the labels on your clothing. Write down every country where each item is made or assembled. Now research how much those making your clothing are being paid, and what their working conditions are. Do you have a sense that you are "robbing" someone, if not God?

3

Chapter Three

The Meaning of Stuff

I'm a lousy confidant. I can't keep a secret worth a hoot. I always spill the beans too soon. And so just to get it over with, I'm going to tell you the best secret I know, the secret to contentment. Here it is: "Contentment is found in knowing that what things mean has nothing to do with who you are."

Things do mean something after all. In our culture we've all learned that money means security, choice, and power. We all have been taught from junior high on that a car means maturity, freedom, and popularity. And all adult males know that different cars mean different things. A Mazda Miata is a "chick" car, at least that's what Click and Clack, the Tappet brothers say—so a real man wouldn't be caught dead in one of those. But a BMW Z-3, now that's a man's car. And a Ford F-250 with a 10-cylinder Cummins diesel engine, well, we won't even try to guess at what that means. But I assure you, it does mean something.

Clothes mean something too. The plain dress of the Amish and other conservative religious sects certainly means something. I live near Lima, Ohio, and when I drive down Watkins Road to the shopping area I often see women working in their gardens in long dresses with long sleeves, and men mowing lawns in white shirts and black vests. Those clothes mean that this family is a member of the German Baptist Brethren congregation down the road. Dunkards (as they're commonly known) dress like that.

Likewise, on teenage girls spaghetti strap tank tops and hip-hugger jeans mean something to teenage boys, if nothing more than "please look at me!" I raised two girls, and I used to be a boy myself; I know what clothes mean. When I was fifteen I had a pair of really cool "engineer boots" and a brown leather jacket. Thinking back, I don't know what—or if—my parents were thinking when they let me wear that stuff to school. A leather jacket and engineer boots meant only one thing in 1957: "tough guy"!

Things do mean something. And that's not all bad. Cars can mean freedom; money can mean choice; and clothes can mean, "I am a modest person." But when things take on the wrong meaning, then you have a problem. And it's a spiritual problem. For example, if you think that by owning or driving or wearing a certain thing makes you something better than what God made you, you've got a problem. Actually, you have two problems.

The first problem is idolatry. When we want to become someone other than who God made us, we idolize whatever that something else is. We might idolize Britney Spears or Calvin Klein or Michael Jordan or anyone else that we would rather be than ourselves. In doing so, we tell God that He made a mistake, that His creation of us was faulty, and that we know better than Him when it comes to who we should be. Hey, want to make God mad? Try it if you want, but don't stand next to me.

The second problem with trying to be "better" than God made you by owning the right stuff is that it just doesn't work. Trying to be more than we are by owning or wearing or having something doesn't work because there's no end to it. Someone else always has more. We can always find someone who looks more like Britany, someone who has more money, someone who owns a bigger house, or someone who drives a cooler car. That's the power that drives consumerism: you never quite have enough to be strong. So you need to buy more.

In Philippians 4:13, which we looked in the last chapter, Paul says that it is Christ who strengthens us, not stuff. I am somebody because Jesus loved me so much that He was willing to die for me. And there isn't anything stronger than a love that leads one to die for another. You might be dying to own a Z-3, or a Miata, but that Miata won't die for you. You might be dying to wear a leather jacket, but that jacket won't die for you. And you might be dying to live in a spectacular home, but that spectacular home won't die for you either.

In fact, the opposite is often true. That Miata or the leather jacket or that spectacular home might just kill you. Buying things to help you be somebody will certainly kill you spiritually. It takes an enormous amount of energy and time, not to mention money. Trying to be somebody through the stuff you own takes away from the development of your faith in Jesus Christ. Jesus wants to be Lord of all of your life, and asking Him to give you eternal life but depending on stuff to give you popularity isn't going to work. The problem isn't just divided loyalty, the problem is that neither Jesus nor stuff likes the competition. Your spiritual life will be killed by the conflict within you.

What kind of spiritual relationship can you have with stuff, anyway? We all know people who just love their car, or just love their house. And we've all heard one woman say to another, " I just love your hair." But this kind of love only goes one way. No matter how often you wash and wax and vacuum your car, it does not have the ability to love you back. And no matter how much your spectacular house is worth, or how much your neighbors envy it, your house cannot love you back.

This is the problem that Paul referred to back in Romans when he said that God "gave the unbelievers over to the lusts of their hearts, for they exchanged the truth of God for a lie, and worshiped and served the creature rather than the Creator" (Romans 1:25). The lie is that things can be a replacement for God. There's that idolatry again: trying to be somebody by stuff is worshipping the creature—the created order—rather than the creator.

We persist in worshipping stuff, even when the evidence shows us our foolishness. In a recent news release it was disclosed that the John Deere Corporation is now going to be selling their lawn mowers in Home Depot stores. This breaks a long-standing tradition of only selling their equipment in their dealer network. The really interesting thing in the news release was the announcement that despite the decreasing average lawn size, the desired horsepower for mowing those smaller lawns is actually increasing. John Coffman, product manager for tractors for Sears' Craftsman equipment, said that this is due to "horsepower envy." He said, "We hear, 'the neighbor has a 15 (horsepower tractor), I want a 16!'" My, what we won't do to be "somebody"!

Bottom line? God hates competition. Think of it. What a blow to be replaced in the hearts of your creatures by something from your own creation. So the secret to being content is not in having it all or in being oblivious to one's own needs, but in putting stuff in its place. Stuff can be good, but stuff is not God. Stuff does not make us important or powerful or popular. It is the love of God in Jesus Christ that makes us somebody. It is the love of God in Jesus Christ that tells us we are indeed loved—loved so much that while we were still sinners He proved His love for us by sending His Son to die for us. What greater proof can there be of our relationship with God than that?

Study Questions

1. Money talks, and everything has meaning. I think my fifteen-year-old Volvo says that I'm a "thrifty" person. What does your stuff say about you? List your more obvious stuff on a sheet of paper and then write down what you want it to say about you.

2. What can you identify in your life that has the potential to take the place of God? Are there occasions when you made a choice and later wonder what God thinks about what you've chosen?

4

Chapter Four

Influences on Our Ideas About Stuff

I'm not sure exactly, but I think it was James Dean who told me that wearing engineer boots and a leather jacket to school meant I was one tough hombre. Well, he didn't exactly tell me, but I got the idea from a movie I'd seen when I was a teenager, Rebel Without a Cause. Movies, TV, and magazines probably have more to do with our understanding of what stuff means than any other influence. Think about it, where did you get the idea that your salary is an indication of your importance, or that the car you drive is a clue to your income? You weren't born with those ideas, you learned them somewhere. The good news is that if we learned that something means something, then we can learn something else about something. The point here is not just that things mean something, but that we're free to change our minds about what things mean.

After all, some of the meanings we've learned do make sense. If your house means hospitality, you probably learned that from your parents, your faith, or even your own experience. And if your clothes mean that you belong to a particular group, like the Amish, then you learned that from the teachings of that group. If a car means freedom and popularity, you probably learned that as a teenager from your peers. And if money means choice, then you probably went through a time in your life when you didn't have much of either. Experience is a great teacher. But to be truthful, a lot of meanings we assign to things come straight from the people who want to sell us those things.

It's time for a confession. For the past thirty years I've had a subscription to New Yorker magazine. It's a great weekly magazine with the best analytical reporting anywhere, easily the best cartoons in print, and usually a good fiction offering each week. The only thing I don't like about the New Yorker is the advertising, most of which is what you might call upscale. It hypes things that interest those for whom money is no object. Moet champagne, British Airways First Class, Tiffany Jewelers, and more investment management services for the wealthy than you can shake a hundred-dollar bill at.

But this advertising does one good thing. Assuming it wouldn't be there unless it worked, it tells me a lot about the mind of the typical American consumer. Looking at the advertising in the New Yorker (or almost any other American magazine for that matter) gives a clear view into the mind and aspirations of its readers. A recent issue to come to my home is a great example.

On the inside of the front cover of the Feb 10, 2003 issue is a five page, glossy, fold-out announcement of the arrival of the new 315-horsepower FX45, Infiniti's version of the SUV. The first two pages are filled with the following words in large print gold on a black background:

"renegade, fearless, unexpected, bold, true, spontaneous, curious, intriguing, unwavering, rare, brash, provocative, intuitive, genuine, daring, uncommon, irreverent, brazen, absolute, unusual, visionary, idyllic, proud, maverick, wild, undaunted, resolute, poetic, dynamic, soulful, unconventional, strong, romantic, authentic, brave, unorthodox, deft, radical, dreamer"

And then, when you unfold the opposite page to uncover a picture of the car itself, you see the words, "You are. It is."

The message is that if you buy this car, you'll be seen as a renegade, fearless, unexpected, and so on. Whoever designed this ad clearly intends that the viewer identify with this car. The sad truth is that this ad is not trying to find people who are already renegades, fearless, bold, etc. This ad is designed to appeal to the unrealized ego desires of the viewer. People will buy this car because they want to be identified with those characteristics, not because they already have them.

The deceitful thing about this ad is that you don't even have to see the car to want to be identified with the gold words it claims to represent. The words themselves appeal to people who are unsure of who they are who'd like to be seen as "somebody." You might actually be more attracted by not seeing a picture of the car, since it looks a lot like a mini-van that's been sat on by an elephant. In my opinion, a good word to head that list of words would be "blind."

The consuming public is repeatedly subjected to one ego-satisfying message after another from an industry whose job it is to induce us to buy their products. And they do that because it works! Why does it work? Humans are born with two big unanswered questions. The first one is, "Am I loved?" The second is, "Am I important?" Almost everything that's available to wear, drive, live in, purchase, or use is advertised by playing on its perceived ability to provide an affirmative answer to one of those two questions.

We learn early on to discern how much we're loved and how important we are by the amount of attention we receive from others. It's an appropriate lesson to learn. An infant who isn't attended to by his mother needs that love so badly that he'll cry and cry until he gets that attention. A young child who's ignored by her parents will act up and misbehave until she gets punished. After all, punishment is attention. Even negative attention is better than none at all. An adult who's not nurtured by his or her peers will often engage in deviant behavior just to get attention.

The question, "Am I loved?" probably produces more anxiety in normal humans than any other question ever asked. God knows that—thus the cross of Jesus Christ. Jesus himself said it this way, "Greater love has no one than this, that one lay down his life for his friends" (John 15:13). That's exactly what Jesus did for us, all of us. What more evidence do we need that we're loved?

But what about being important? What's so important about being important? Up pops the ego again. Something about being human makes us rate ourselves in terms of importance.

I fly a lot these days, often a couple trips a week. Because the airlines want my business, they try to make me feel important by giving me special privileges through an elite club called "Premier Status." I admit that when they seat me in First Class after I've only paid for a coach seat and then give me a hot cup of coffee as soon as I'm seated, I feel pretty important. But on a recent trip I learned a new way of being "important."

My seat mate and I were having a conversation about the number of people talking on their cell phones while waiting for the airplane doors to be closed. We discussed how some of them were almost shouting into their phones, as if to let the rest of us know how important they were. I told my companion that I solved the problem of irritating others on the plane by getting rid of my cell phone. She asked me, "But how does your office get in touch with you?" When I replied that they get in touch with me when I call them, she replied, "Boy, you must really be important." Isn't it amazing how the meaning of importance changed from seeming important if you had a cell phone to being really important if you didn't have a cell phone.

Even in the church, being important is important. You've seen how books on spiritual subjects are advertised and sold today. The subject of the book often isn't what sells it, but the importance of the author. "Authored by America's most influential pastor," the magazine ad says. "Written by best selling author so-and-so," the book jacket says. And on the promotional posters in Christian bookstores: "From the founder of the world's fastest growing church!"

Why do we worship celebrities? What is it about famous people that attracts our attention and devotion? Frankly, I'm not sure, but I wish we could get over it because I'm tired of being betrayed by them. It seems to be a rule of celebrity that as soon as one gets to be really well known, he or she does something that brings them back down to earth with the rest of us sinners. Sometimes it's sexual, sometimes it's just stupid, but most of the time it has something to do with that most essential piece of stuff on earth, money! Even William Bennett, past U.S. Secretary of Education, Drug Czar, and author of books on virtue was discredited by published evidence and his own admission of a high-stakes gambling habit.

When celebrities actually live up to their image of importance, what does it do for us? On my last trip a large, well-dressed African American man got on the plane late and sat down next to me. Immediately the woman in the row in front of me turned and said to him, "Let me say that I really enjoy watching you box." The man thanked her for the compliment. I had no idea who the man was, besides now knowing he was a boxer. It wasn't until someone called him Mr. Holyfield that I realized I was sitting next to Evander Holyfield, the heavyweight boxer. The funny thing was that I was the only one near him who didn't want his autograph. I couldn't think of any reason to have it. I don't think that having Evander Holyfield's autograph would make me more loved or more important. As well-known as he may be, his importance made little difference to me. However, that apparently wasn't true of many other people on the plane!

My two unanswered questions are, "Why do Christians need to be important?" and "Why do we worship those we think are important?" What could add more importance than having the only sinless man on earth die for your salvation? How could a car, even a 315-horsepower FX45 make one more important than that? And why would you worship anyone other than the one who was willing to die for you?

Study Questions

1. Who told you that money meant security? What discussions did you have about money with your parents? How much of what you know about money have you learned from example rather than an overt lesson?

2. How do you feel about the meaning that Madison Avenue attaches to things? For example, to me the only thing buying the new Infinity SUV means is that the buyer has very poor taste in cars. But I agree with the advertising that tells me the Mini-Cooper is a fun car to drive—it sure looks like fun!

3. Who would you ask for an autograph if you had the opportunity? What would you do with that autograph? Who are your "heroes"? Who are the celebrities in your universe of important people?

5

Chapter Five

The Trouble With Stuff

I'm not paranoid, but I'm suspicious that somebody is watching me. They must be. How else would Volvo know, for example, that in 1993 I had just decided that I had found the perfect car for me, their 240 DL sedan. Why else would they stop producing the 240 DL sedan in 1994? And General Motors must be watching me as well, because just as soon as I had decided that I had found the next perfect car for me, the Geo Prism, they stopped producing them too. Actually, GM never really produced the Prism; they bought the frames, drive trains, and electronics from Toyota, put a slightly different body and a Chevy emblem on each one, and sold them as Geo's. But the point remains, as soon as I found a car I really liked, the automobile industry stopped producing it. Somebody is watching me.

It's called "planned obsolescence." The whole point of it

is to keep one step ahead of the consumer. That's the problem with buying something to gain status or to project an image of importance. As soon as you climb to the top of the image heap by buying a new car, your car becomes a used car. And before you know it, a new model appears in the showroom—a new model that's just different enough from your model that your image is now "out of date." That's what I liked about the Volvo 240 DL—they hardly ever changed it.

Fleeting status is not the only problem with trying to be loved or important by owning stuff. Sometimes it works the other way around. In 1991 I inherited my father's 1957 Mercedes 219S, a nice, old, roomy, dark green European sedan. It was the kind of car that you open the door, walk in, close the door, and then go sit down. Well, not really, but it sure seemed like that.

My father bought the car in 1959 when we were living in France. When the family returned to the US, he shipped it home to California, and he continued to drive it for the next 20 years. The odometer quit at 350,000 miles, but he still drove the car. A few years later the 30 year-old key broke off in the ignition switch, but he wired around the switch and kept driving the car. Then, in the late 1980s, when the car had over 500,000 miles on it, Dad bought a four-wheel drive SUV to get up the dirt road to the mountainside where he was building a house. And the Mercedes got parked.

In 1991 my brother called and asked if I wanted the Mercedes. He told me that Dad and Mom were moving down from the mountain and they needed to get the car off the property. He said that if I wanted the car, it was mine. I'm not terribly nostalgic, but having your father's antique Mercedes at no cost other than the gas it would take to get it back to Ohio was hard to turn down. So I flew to California to get the car. I drove it to Eugene, Oregon, for a conference I was attending, and then headed east across the Cascades toward Ohio. I had been on some great road trips in the 60s, but this was the best road trip I'd ever been on!

The first thing I noticed was that for 2,000 miles I had great posture. Four days of sitting up straight will do wonders for your back—and for your ego! After all, you tend to sit up when you're being noticed. And boy, was I being noticed! Cars would pass me going 80 miles an hour, hit the brakes, slow up till they were back even with me, and then give the old Mercedes a good looking-over. Some even gave me a "thumbs up" sign, which I took to mean, "nice car." It was kind of fun being noticed because of the car I was driving.

However, that all changed. When I drove through my hometown, all of a sudden it wasn't fun anymore. In fact it got downright unpleasant. Same car, same me, but a very different reaction. Instead of the "nice-car" look, what I got from people who knew me was the, "who-does-he-think-he-is?" look. Driving that car still had meaning, but the meaning became negative instead of positive. The people I lived among thought I was "stuck up," not "up scale." And that nice old car that I had paid absolutely nothing for suddenly became a problem. It projected an image, but not the one I wanted.

That's the other problem with stuff: you can't control what it means. Sometimes it works for you, sometimes against you. Among my circle of friends, nothing has more status than a 20-year-old Volvo. We are the "simple living" advocates of our generation. "Making do" is a spiritual virtue in our value system. I've never told my friends that the car I'd really like to own is a 1952 XK120 Jaguar with a British racing green body, leather seats, and a convertible top! What a car! But can you imagine the problem I'd have if I drove a Jaguar into the parking lot of a Conservative

Mennonite church and then tried to preach about "steward-ship"? Not a good idea!

Clothes can create a similar problem. In my work I speak to both ends of the social spectrum. In rural Kansas I'm almost always overdressed when I show up in a jacket and tie. But in eastern Pennsylvania I am usually underdressed in that same jacket and tie. However, there are places in eastern Pennsylvania where if I wear a tie at all I am way overdressed. For example, in 1987 I went to a community near Chambersburg, Pennsylvania to speak to at a missions conference. I wore my recently purchased maroon sports coat and the flowery tie that came with it.

I arrived early at the auditorium and took a seat in the front row with my host. We chatted for awhile, not paying much attention to the crowd gathering behind us. About an hour into the conference session, I was introduced and called up to the lectern. When I stepped to the podium I arranged my notes, took a deep breath, looked out over the audience, and opened my mouth to begin speaking. But what I saw before I said anything changed drastically what I said.

I was going to say that I was glad to be there in front of them and honored by the invitation, but the first part of that sentence would've been a bald-faced lie! For at that moment I wasn't glad to be there at all; in fact I was horribly embarrassed! Sitting in front of me were approximately 300 people from some of the most conservative religious groups in the area, "plain" people. They were all looking at me as if I were from outer space! And in their terms, I really was from another planet. In that auditorium were 300 people dressed in white, gray, and black, and one person in a red sports coat with a flowered tie!

Believe me, clothes mean something, but you can't always determine what they mean. At least not right away. I told the assembled group that I was sorry but that I was new to the region and did not know about their dress code. That seemed to reduce the tension in the room somewhat. But then I did the most brilliant thing I've ever done: I also told them the truth that I had gotten the jacket and tie on sale! You would've thought I had just offered to take them off and burn them! "Don't worry," they seemed to say, "if you got them on sale, you must be one of us!"

Wearing stylish clothes can either mean that you're important or impertinent, depending on where you wear them. Driving an expensive car can mean that you have good taste or a poor sense of economics, depending on where you drive it. A house the size of a small community college can mean that you're unbelievably hospitable or that you're unbelievably selfish—depending on how you use it. The point I'm emphasizing is that stuff means something. The stuff we own can add to or subtract from our lives, depending on our context and our intentions. Sadly, many of the meanings we assign to stuff are precisely what drive our need to possess it.

But remember: if we learned somewhere that stuff means something, we can also unlearn it! We're not condemned to believe forever that any particular thing means what we were told about it on TV. We're free to change our minds about what things mean.

That brings up the next question in our journey to contentment: How do we decide what things mean?

Study Questions

1. Think back and identify a situation in which the meaning you attached to a particular thing wasn't perceived that way by someone else. For example, I thought that driving the classic Mercedes Benz automobile that I inherited from my father would mean that I was a connoisseur of fine cars. However, to some in the community I served as a pastor it meant that I had placed myself above them.

2. When have circumstances made you change the meaning you had attached to something? For example, did the bursting of the "tech-bubble" change the meaning of investing for you?

3. What meaning-of-stuff issues might you need to address in your life right now?

6

Chapter Six

Inherent Usefulness

Since someone else always has a bigger house or a newer car or a larger salary than we have, the idea of stuff meaning status or image doesn't really work very well. And since stuff doesn't have to mean what our society or the media says it means, we can decide how the meaning of stuff might work for us instead of against us. For example, if a car no longer means status or image, what might it mean that would be more appropriate for us? This brings up the concept of inherent usefulness.

What's a car inherently useful for? What basic problem or concern in our lives does a car solve? I don't know about anybody else's life, but a car solves a basic problem in my life, and that's the need to get to the airport on time. For me, a car's inherent usefulness is based on needing reliable transportation. Reliability is something you can accurately measure. Reliability comes with history, and some cars are historically more reliable than others. According to Consumer Reports, probably the most trusted and reliable advisor on consumer issues, the Toyota Corolla and Honda Civic drive trains (engine, transmission, axles, etc.) have the lowest maintenance costs per mile in automobile history. Take note that none of this reliability has anything to do with what the cars look like or what I look like in them.

Another inherent usefulness to be found in a car is pleasure—at least for some people. Some people enjoy driving, and some cars are more fun to drive than others. When I had to drive from my home in West Liberty, Ohio, to Holmes and Wayne County churches, I always took Route 3 through the countryside instead of taking the interstate, I-71. The freeway was actually quicker, but Route 3 was a lot more fun, especially in my Volvo 240 DL. That car took the curves like they belonged to it! And even with a four-cylinder engine, it loved the hills. The part of that drive that I enjoyed the most was the part that passed for mountains in Ohio, between Loudenville and Mount Vernon. But only in the Volvo. Other cars I've driven on that highway weren't nearly as fun to drive.

Likewise, a house has inherent usefulness apart from what it looks like, how big it is, or how much it's worth. Comfort, security, and potential for hospitality are all values that make a house useful. Of course you could get carried away with any of those. So you have to ask how much comfort or how much security do I need? Or how much hospitality should I be able to offer?

That brings us to another of those counter-culture things: how do you decide what you need? The world says you need everything you can afford. A recent best seller in the financial world, The Millionaire Next Door, proposes that the higher your income is while you're working, the more you'll need to retire on. There is a relationship between what you spend now and what you will spend then, but that relationship is not dependent on what your income is at any time. It is dependent on what your needs are. You don't need everything you can afford.

However, not everyone thinks that way. For example, it's common for people who inherent money to go out and buy all new furniture for their home. Did having that money instantly make their old furniture shabbier? No, I don't think so. Likewise, getting a raise at work doesn't mean that you should go out and buy a bigger car. After all, you aren't going to carry the extra money around in the trunk, so you don't really need a bigger trunk, do you? The thinking that says you need everything you can afford is one of the most destructive myths ever perpetuated.

But we do need things. And God wants our needs to be met. In 2 Corinthians 9:8, for example, we read that "God's grace abounds so much, that having everything you need, you have an abundance for every good work."

The reason God wants your needs to be met is obvious. If your needs are not being met, you're not going to be helping meet others' needs. If you're living with a tree for your only shelter, you probably aren't volunteering with Habitat For Humanity to help someone else build a house. If you're hungry, you're probably not donating food to your local food bank. And so on. So it's important to have your needs met.

So if "all you can afford" isn't the way to measure need, what is? Let me suggest that you need everything and every service necessary for living out God's call in your life. Life has a purpose, and it isn't the pursuit of happiness—it's the fulfillment of God's call. So what is God's call for you? I don't know that, so I can't tell you what your needs are.

I can suggest, however, that God's call has something to

do with the inherent usefulness of life itself. Take a look at the animal kingdom. What does life seem to mean in terms of inherent usefulness for a deer or a mountain lion, for example? What do they seem to do mostly? How about eat, breed, and eat some more? The inherent usefulness of the lives of animals is to reproduce themselves so that the balance in nature is maintained. So what about humans, what inherent usefulness will help us define what our needs are?

What if we decided that reproduction is our inherent usefulness as well? After all, doesn't God's call in scripture have something to do with "making disciples of all nations"? Aren't we to reproduce ourselves in that way, as well as in the more biological way? To do that we must have certain needs met. The basic needs are obvious, like food, water, shelter, clothing, and transportation. Still other needs are essential to the reproduction of Christians. Like dating for example.

Dating? Sure. In our culture if you never date, you won't reproduce very many of yourself biologically. Not everyone is called to be married, but if you don't keep dating while you're married, the two of you are going to need twice as much housing someday, and that's not very useful reproduction. Recreation is another need that's essential for living out God's call. If you're not "re-created" every once in a while, you'll burn out and stop reproducing.

We have lots of other essential needs. But they're all best determined by their inherent usefulness in helping us fulfill God's call in our lives—not by whether we can afford them or not.

So what's the inherent usefulness of the stuff in our lives? A car has inherent usefulness in its mechanical ability to move us around; a house has inherent usefulness in its ability to give us space to live. Money, however, does not have any inherent usefulness beyond the meaning we give it. Think about it, a five-dollar bill isn't big enough or soft enough to wipe your nose with, or anything else for that matter. A credit card can be used to scrape ice off your windshield, but that's not what it was designed to do.

Money is only useful if we believe that it has value. That's why that the American dollar can be bought for about 120 Yen at the moment; the Japanese don't think that our dollar has much value. It works the other way as well. The Canadian dollar is weak compared to our dollar—right now it's worth only about two thirds as much. Why? We don't think that their dollar is worth as much as ours. When it comes to money, inherent usefulness can be quite subjective.

Money does have a certain consistent inherent usefulness. For example, money is often described as a medium of exchange. It's actually pretty useful. It would be a real pain to have to trade corn for groceries, for example. Think of the hassle it would be if you had to take a bushel of corn to the store to trade for a gallon of milk. The grocery store would need an enormous storage facility for all the corn. So money is inherently useful as a medium of exchange.

Money also is inherently useful because it gives us something else that's measurable: choice. When you don't have money in our "market" society, you don't have many choices. Money can bring freedom—the ability to go where and when you want to, and to do what you want to. Money can even bring security—to a point.

I've noticed in my seminars that when I ask what money means, the first answer I get is usually "security." But then someone in one of my workshops piped up and said, "only to a point!" He told how insecure his family was when they didn't have enough money, and how secure they felt when they finally had enough money to meet their needs. As their income and net worth rose over the years, though, instead of feeling more secure they began to feel insecure again. They discovered that money only means security when you have "enough."

Not having enough money brings the insecurity of not knowing where your next meal is coming from or how you're going to pay the rent next month. But when you have more money than you need, you start to worry about safe places to put it: "Should we be in bonds? What if the bank goes bust? Who do we trust to handle our investments?" When things were going so wonderfully in the stock market, the question being asked was "Which company's stock will increase in value the most?" Since the "tech-bubble" burst, that question has been replaced by, "Which company's stock will not go bust because of management greed?" All these questions are driven by insecurity.

Even if money does mean security, more money does not make you more secure. The most powerful thing about contentment is knowing when enough is enough!

Study Questions

1. Can you identify the "inherent usefulness" of the things you own? Take an inventory and make a list of the things you own, and then next to each thing write down its inherent usefulness.

2. If someone asked you to describe your "calling" in life, what would you say?

7

Chapter Seven

The Power of Enough

I recently received a letter from a consumers' buying club in Fort Wayne, Indiana. In the envelope with the letter was a car key and a brochure describing prizes that I was guaranteed to win if I just came to their store and listened to a sales presentation designed to convince me to join their buyers' club. First prize was a brand new Mercury Cougar, and the letter promised that if the key in my envelope turned in the ignition and started the car, the car was mine! The other prizes were a new Broyhill bedroom furniture suite, a new Kawasaki four-wheeler, $1000 cash, $300 cash, and finally, a free vacation. The vacation consisted of two nights in a condo in Orlando or Las Vegas, but you had to get there on your own. The letter said that I was guaranteed to win one of the prizes.

About a week later I got a phone call from a lady at the

store asking me to make an appointment to come and pick up my "guaranteed prize." I was sort of busy working on a writing project, and without thinking much about it I replied that I had looked at the list of prizes and had come to the conclusion that I didn't want any of them.

After a bit of a pause, the woman on the other end of the line said, "Now Mr. Miller, surely you would want an extra $300 cash." Reading right off the page that I was developing at the time, I used a variation of the response I described using with a tele-marketer in the introduction of this book: "No thank you, I have enough cash, and more cash couldn't possibly make me happier." Without saying a word, she hung up! And that's when I realized the power of "enough." You can't argue with someone who has enough. Madison Avenue has no power over people who have enough.

Since that time, I've wanted to meet that woman and ask her what she thought I meant when I said I had "enough cash." After all, I could have meant that I have more money than I can count, and just a measly $300 wouldn't make a difference. But I don't have anywhere near that much money, and I could surely give away another $300. I don't "have it all" in financial terms, but I have sufficient money to worship with, meet my needs, and have some extra for more giving. And that's the key word in finding contentment, sufficiency.

In the ninth chapter of his second letter to the Corinthians, the Apostle Paul says that "God is able to make all grace abound to you, that always having all sufficiency in everything, you may have an abundance for every good deed" (2 Corinthians 9:8, NASB). I take this to mean that God is so generous that not only will we have enough for ourselves, we also will have more for the good works that God will send our way. Enough and more! The whole verse is amazing, but the middle phrase is the most amazing of all.

Three absolutes in one little phrase: "always having all sufficiency in everything." Enough isn't just the bare minimum once in a while, it's having all sufficiency in every thing, always!

A little later in the same letter, Paul reveals that he has something wrong in his life that he calls a "thorn in the flesh." He identifies is as a "messenger of Satan," given to him to keep him from exalting himself. Although he recognizes its presence as something to help him in his Christian walk, it's still inconvenient or painful enough that he prays three times for it to be removed. But God's reply says, "My grace is sufficient for you, for my power is perfected in weakness" (2 Corinthians 12:9). This surprising connection between strength and enough comes straight from God. "You have enough of what you need to handle this problem," God seems to be saying, "and by handling it this way you will display a different kind of power." Having enough does not mean having it all, but it does mean having what is needed to get the job done.

The other possible meaning of my "I have enough" statement might be that I'm determined to "hunker-down and do without," something like financial dieting. However, having enough is not at all like dieting. Way too many "financial freedom" plans are based on the two principles of dieting, avoidance and deprivation. That's why dieting doesn't work, at least not for very many people for very long. Negative results seldom have the power to motivate. That's probably why North American culture has the lowest savings rate of any industrialized nation on earth. "Delayed gratification" for most Americans is no gratification at all. One of the least effective sales pitches for savings that I know of is the one that shows the dramatic amount that a modest savings deposit is worth to a high school graduate 45 years down the road.

Now avoidance is a good thing when it comes to dangerous stuff, like rattlesnakes, cliff edges, and things that are addictive—like drugs and pornography. But trying to be content by avoiding something is like trying to be well fed by not eating. Fasting has its place, but in nutritional terms it cannot take the place of a full stomach. In fact, evidence suggests that avoiding something only makes one's appetite for it sharper. And likewise, indulgence can dull the desire for some things.

Deprivation is also a poor motivator for change. For example, it's difficult to convince poor people to live simply, for simple living is really available only to those who have the choice not to do so. The difference between poverty and simple living is just that: choice. Those who are deprived have nothing else to choose.

Having enough does not mean gritting your teeth and putting up with what you have. "Doing without" is not a spiritual virtue anymore than "doing well" is. But defining what something means in terms of its inherent usefulness and then deciding what "enough" means by using that definition gives you the "power of enough" and the satisfied feeling that comes with having neither too little nor too much. It's like being neither hungry nor stuffed, just pleasantly full. And that is power.

The only real motivating force that Madison Avenue has is anxiety. If the luxury car you drive displays your status to the rest of the world, then the sight of a newer luxury car in someone else's driveway creates the anxiety that perhaps someone else has higher status or importance than you. Likewise, if the size of the house you own or the size of the lot it sits on indicates your level of importance in the community, the next new house that's larger creates anxiety that you've just been lowered in the community hierarchy.

Knowing when "enough is enough" is the antidote to that

kind of anxiety. When you know that, Madison Avenue loses its power to convince you to buy a newer car or a larger house in your desperate drive to reduce the anxiety in your life. The size of your house or the age of your car compared to someone else's no longer produces anxiety. Comparison is the source of most of our anxieties.

Every year financial magazines run salary comparison surveys. The implication to the reader begins with the question, "Are you being paid as much as these important people are?" If so, then congratulations, you must be as important as they are. If you aren't, then you ought to be paid more. But why should what someone else makes have anything to do with me? I make enough money for my needs, and more money will not make me work any harder. However, the natural human tendency is to compare oneself with others. Even the apostles were caught comparing themselves to each other.

Perhaps the first step in setting yourself free from this debilitating habit is deciding to whom you should compare yourself. For example, if I compare my salary to other professionals in our nation with equal experience and education, I don't measure up very well. But if I compare myself to my peers in other parts of the world, I'm sitting pretty close to the top of the heap. The second step is the one that will set you free from the anxiety that comes with not measuring up. That step is to compare your income with your needs. If there's any truth to God's statement that not only will he meet your needs but that you'll also have more for good works, then you'll always come out a winner.

Study Questions

1. When have you realized that you had enough of something? What feeling accompanied that realization?

2. In what areas of your life do you sense that you just "don't measure up?" By what standard are you measuring?

3. In what ways do you practice "delayed gratification" in your daily life. For example, do you eat the cake first and save the frosting for last? How do you eat Oreo's?

8
Chapter Eight

What You Really Need

The intent of the salary-comparison articles I mentioned earlier is to encourage you to compare your salary against that of your peers. They attempt to give you a measurement to enable you to answer the question, "am I being paid enough?"

However, if you no longer equate your salary with your professional status, and if money is simply something that gives you the ability to make the choices you want to make in your life, then comparing your salary against someone else's is like comparing apples to oranges. They are both fruit but they have very different tastes and purposes in the menu of life.

A few societies in the world perceive money as having little inherent usefulness, such as the Basarwa people in Botswana. Normally called "Bushmen" by tourists, the few remaining Basarwa live in the middle of the Kalahari Desert, where they survive by hunting game and gathering roots and wild vegetables. Cash has little appeal to them for there's little that they need that they must buy, and almost no place in the Kalahari to buy it. In our three years in Botswana we were impressed by the "ecological affluence" enjoyed by those members of the society who were primarily self-sufficient in terms of producing their own food and building their own dwellings.

The nearer the Basarwa culture edges to the city and to employment, the more cash the people have in their pockets but the less time they have to raise their own food or build their own houses. In their case, the more cash they have, the fewer choices they have: earning cash means that they have to sell their labor rather than spend their time producing what they need.

In our society money is the common medium of exchange, the intermediary between our labor and the fulfilling of our needs. So we do need money to meet our needs. But how much money? Society seems to say that we need everything we can afford, or everything our neighbor has, or everything the media says we deserve—plus a little more. That's why we have so much consumer debt.

If you think about it, needing everything you can afford is a pretty silly way to define a need. Just because your children's college tuition is paid and you have more disposable income than you've ever have had, that doesn't mean you "need" a newer, bigger house—especially now that you have fewer people to live in it. Needing everything your neighbor has is equally silly—your neighbor isn't you and doesn't have your needs. Likewise, needing what the media says you deserve is a bit of a stretch since the media doesn't have the faintest idea who you are.

However, we do have needs, and most of them require

money to be satisfied. The best way to know what your needs are is to keep track of them. That might seem a little obsessive to those of us who are used to just spending the money until it runs out. But if you think about it, keeping a record of where your money goes is just a matter of good management. There are few more anxiety-producing feelings than realizing that despite your nice salary you haven't the faintest idea where all the money went.

For a typical person/family a list of needs might look like this:
- Charitable contributions (placed first because of their worship significance)
- Cash contingency savings ("rainy day" funds to replace refrigerator, fix auto transmission, etc)
- Loans/Savings (loan payments that become savings deposits after the loan is paid off)
- Recreation/Dating (a marriage relationship that is not nurtured soon demands higher housing expense)
- Housing rent or mortgage (you can't live in a mutual fund or CD)
- Home Insurance
- Real Estate Taxes
- Repairs
- Utilities
- Telephone
- Water
- Food
- Dining out / Carry in
- Household consumables (cleaning/paper supplies, etc)
- Clothing
- Transportation (fuel, regular maintenance)
- Car Repairs
- Fees (registration, license plates, etc)

- Car Insurance
- Travel (airfare, lodging, food, etc)
- Healthcare
- Dental care
- Health Insurance
- Personal care services (haircuts, etc)
- Personal care items (shoe polish, shampoo)
- Hobbies
- Gifts
- Taxes (Income, sales, other)
- Miscellaneous

Unfortunately, this list doesn't tell you how much is enough of any of these things. And that brings up the real definition of what a need is. God has a plan for those He has saved. And that plan is to be involved in the salvation of others. Ephesians 2:7 probably says it the best, we are saved "so that in the age to come He might display (through us) the surpassing riches of his kindness toward us in Christ Jesus." A need, therefore, is some thing or some service that's essential in the fulfillment of that calling to be a display of "the surpassing riches of His kindness toward us in Christ Jesus." Before every purchase or every commitment of time, ask yourself if this thing or service will help you display the surpassing riches of God's kindness towards you. Another question might be, "Will this help me or anyone else be a better follower of Jesus Christ, or will it just get in the way?"

So if need is dependent on calling, how much money is enough? If your calling is to be hospitable by offering housing and meals to strangers, then you'll probably need a bit more money for housing and food. If your calling is to be involved in transporting the elderly to their doctor's visits, then you'll probably need a little larger vehicle—easier to get in and out of—and a little more money for gasoline and maintenance than otherwise. And if your calling is to make your skills available to persons in other cultures, you'll probably need a little more money for travel expenses.

One of the best ways to begin this journey of deciding how much is enough is to keep track of just what it costs to live the way you currently do. After a year or so, you'll know how much food is going to cost you over a year and how much you'll need for auto expenses or utilities. But even then you have some choices. Other than debt contracts such as house mortgages and car payments, there are really very few "fixed" expenses that we have little choice about. I'll pay the electric bill each month no matter how much it is, and I'll buy gasoline for the car no matter what the price of gasoline is. But I do have a choice about how much electricity I'll use next month, or how much gasoline I'll use next month. Turning the lights out in an unused room, turning down the thermostat and wearing a sweater, combining trips to town, and joining a car pool are all choices that affect how much money is necessary for those "fixed" expenses. In other words, for most "fixed" expenses we have to pay something but how much is up to us.

Even with real fixed expenses we have choices to make. In the case of a house mortgage, for example, we can choose how big a house to buy, what neighborhood it's in, how long to finance it, and even when to refinance to take advantage of lower interest rates. One of the most efficient ways to lower the cost of home ownership is called "front-end loading." This is the practice of getting the longest term mortgage possible—usually 30 years—with the lowest payments and the lowest interest rate, and then making extra payments on the principle whenever possible. One of the best ways to do this is to make the regular monthly payment and then two weeks later make another payment on the principle. This spreads the financial burden throughout the month and allows one to pay only the monthly payment when unexpected expenses occur.

The point of all this is that not only does money mean choice, but that the amount of money needed to live depends on choice as well—the choices we make as we live.

Study Questions

1. Have you ever kept track of your expenses? If you did that, were there any surprises in the monthly or yearly totals?

2. What would you consider to be your "fixed expenses"? And in what areas of your expenditures do you have more latitude?

3. What clever methods have you found to multiply the power of money, such as "front-end loading"?

9

Chapter Nine

Future Funding

Someday I want to be able to receive a paycheck each month without having to fill out a timesheet, write quarterly progress reports, or worry about my employer going out of business or laying me off. Someday I want to be able to write my own paychecks based on my own needs that month. Someday I want to be able to spend time doing something that does not pay for itself; to say "yes" to projects that will have no remuneration. In other words, someday I want to be financially independent.

Normally we call that period of life "retirement." Retirement in our society is usually portrayed as a 20-30 year period of leisure and luxury that doesn't begin until age 65. But if that's what retirement is, I never want to retire. I want to live usefully and pay myself to do so, as soon as I can.

Financial independence is not the same as being independently wealthy, but it is being independently self-sufficient in terms of income. So how much money will be enough to be financially independent? The following "steps" will help you determine how much will be enough for you to be financially independent.

Step 1: Determine annual income needed

First, decide how much income will make you content. Experience shows that retired people tend to spend less than working people, typically about 25% less. But if you plan on extra expenses, you might want to increase that expectation somewhat. My wife and I, for example, plan to spend the first years of our "retirement" exploring the world looking for good examples of sustainable development that we want to support financially. So we're considering spending a little more than we do now, about $2000 per month. At our age and with our employment history, we can expect to receive $800/mo from Social Security. So we need to generate an extra $1200/mo from our own retirement savings.

$1200/month x 12 = $14,400/year retirement income needed from our own resources.

Step 2: Determine expected return rate

Since the extra retirement income you need will come from your own capital, you need to estimate the rate of return (after taxes) you think your capital will provide during those years. Advice from a professional investment counselor is crucial at this point. Higher returns demand higher risk, but fairly safe returns can reasonably be expected to be from 5 to 8 percent. Even in "bear market" years, corporate bond funds return from 4 to 6 percent. For this step I will choose a mid-point, 6.5 percent. Divide your yearly retirement income needs by that rate (6.5 percent equals .065).

$14,400 divided by 0.065 = $ 221,538 capital needed in today's dollars.

Step 3: Determine timeframe until retirement

One of the shocking realities of the world of finance is inflation. Inflation means what it says: something is being inflated, in this case the cost of living. If bread sold for one dollar a loaf this year, I could buy 221,538 loaves of bread with our planned retirement savings. But ten years from now, since the price of bread will inflate, I will get fewer loaves for the same amount of money. The question is how much more money will I need to get the same number of loaves of bread? This is another place where contentment and choice have a big effect on how much is enough.

The U.S. government calculates the inflation rate from the rise in the cost of the items in the typical "market basket" purchased by the typical American consumer. But people who have learned the secret of contentment are not the typical American consumer. We don't buy what the typical American buys, nor do we define our social status on our possessions. We don't buy new houses every five years, new cars every three years, or new computers every two years. Recent research has shown that for those who know how to be content, the average yearly rate of inflation for retired Americans is only 2 percent.

The first task in calculating inflation is to ask what time frame we are planning on. In my case, I want to be financially independent when I am 70 years old, ten years from now. See our example below:

a. At what age do you want to start paying yourself? 70 years old

b. What is your current age? 60 years old

c. Subtract (b) from (a) to get "years until financial independence" 10 years

Step 4: Account for inflation

Now find your inflation factor from the following table (the 2 percent contented, simple living rate) and multiply "capital needed" by it to find your total retirement capital needed.

Years till retirement	Inflation Factor
2	1.04
4	1.08
6	1.13
8	1.17
10	1.22
12	1.27
14	1.32
16	1.37
18	1.43
20	1.49
25	1.64
30	1.81
35	2.0
40	2.21

$ 221,538 X 1.22 = $ 270,276 Total Retirement capital needed

Step 5: Account for interest gain

You're likely thinking, "Wow! How could I ever save over a quarter of a million dollars in ten years? That's a lot of money!" Fortunately, I don't need it right now; I need it ten years into the future. And although inflation makes money worth less in the future, compound interest makes money worth more in the future. Here again you need the advice of a financial professional, but 50 years of investment history have shown us that over the broad range of investments in U.S. markets, 9 percent has been the average rate of return after taxes. From the following list, pick the rate of growth you project for your capital if invested now.

a. aggressive growth (mostly common stocks) 12 percent

b. balanced growth and income (stocks and bonds) 9 percent

c. safety and conservation (mostly bonds & CDs) 6 percent

At my age, I want to be neither very aggressive nor inappropriately conservative, so I'm going to aim for a 9% return over the next ten years. From the following chart find the multiplier for your combination of years to retirement and projected growth rate.

Number of years	Multiplier for 12% expected return	Multiplier for 9% expected return	Multiplier for 6% expected return
2	.7972	.8417	.8900
4	.6355	.7084	.7921
6	.5066	.5963	.7050
8	.4039	.5019	.6274
10	.3220	.4224	.5884
12	.2567	.3555	.4970
14	.2046	.2992	.4423
16	.1631	.2519	.3936
18	.1300	.2120	.3503
20	.1037	.1784	.3118
25	.0588	.1160	.2330
30	.0334	.0754	.1741

And now comes the moment of truth. Multiply this factor by the retirement capital needed to get retirement savings needed now.

.4224 X $ 270,276 = $114,165

That's more like it! And even though I've saved for my

financial independence for only the last 17 years, I now have approximately that much—and it's growing at the average rate of 9 percent per year. That means that from now on, I can choose to simply work for room, board, and health care! It's true, money does mean freedom and choice!

But, you say, "What if I'm not there yet?" "What if I don't have enough so that if I just let it grow until I want to be financially independent there will be enough to pay myself what I want?" There are at least three good ways to achieve this goal:

1. Keep working and saving for your retirement.
2. Increase your risk tolerance.
3. Decrease your income expectations.

Notice that none of these depend on a bull market, a rich uncle, or a winning lottery ticket. They just depend on good planning and following through with the plans. That 's a pretty good definition of stewardship, come to think of it!

Study Questions

1. Do the exercise in this chapter. How much will you need in total capital to achieve the retirement goals you've set for yourself?

2. How much would you need to have saved today so that without saving more you will be financially independent when you want to be?

3. When you get to the point of financial independence, how are you going to give away the rest of your life?

10

Chapter Ten

Saving $115,000 in 17 Years

Americans like being scared. That's the only conclusion I can draw from observing what's popular in our society. Every year someone builds a new roller coaster somewhere in America—one that is faster, higher, and yes, scarier. Every year Hollywood puts out a new crop of horror movies— movies with more blood, more violence, and yes, more scary scenes than the ones last year. One of the most scary things currently being promoted in American society is not a movie about "Chainsaw Charlie" or another Friday the 13th movie; it's a "Free, No Obligation, Retirement Planning Seminar." If you want to really be scared, just go to one of those.

When you're talking about terrorism, a financial planning seminar rates high on the list. Nothing scares people more than what they're told at one of those seminars: that they'll they need millions of dollars in the bank to have a "comfortable retirement"; that this money needs to be protected (at great expense) by a trust or will or something else that will keep the government from taking it all; and that they will never be able to determine how much will be enough! That last part is the scariest thing of all, but it doesn't have to be that way. If you read the previous chapter and did the exercise, that fear should be gone. The good news is that not only can we determine how much we will need, we can also take comfort that we already know how to save it.

Unfortunately, that doesn't mean there isn't anything to be anxious about. For example, I think we should be scared to death at our society's lack of savings discipline. Ask yourself, are you disciplined when it comes to saving for retirement? Here's an even more embarrassing question: If it weren't for the matching funds in your 401K plan or your company's pension plan, how much would you be saving on a regular basis? Oops, that's a very personal question. Our national savings rate gives us the answer. That answer is, "Not much!" We are not a nation of savers, and that should scare us silly.

Back in Chapter 8, the third thing on the list of needs was an item called "loans/savings." You might have wondered why those two things were combined on one line of a spending plan. What I wonder about is why Americans are so good at making payments on consumer loans and so lousy at making savings deposits. We have the highest level of private consumer debt in the industrialized world, and the lowest savings rate. That's baffling, since a loan payment is nothing more than a savings deposit going in the other direction!

Think about it for a minute. The actual physical process of making a loan payment is exactly the same as making a savings deposit, except for one crucial thing: who gets the money. A day or two before the payment is due, you sit down and write out a check for the payment amount, fill out the payment slip that you tore out of the payment book, put both in an envelope, and either mail or take the envelope to the bank. That's exactly what you do to make a savings deposit: write a check, fill out a deposit slip, and send or take both to the bank. It seems like making loan payments is a great way to develop the habit of saving money for financial independence.

At some point early in their adult lives, most Americans borrow money to buy a car, furniture, or some other consumer product. But most don't feel very good about it. In fact, popular financial advisors have found that the biggest attraction for their advice and products is the promise of "debt-free living." It's almost a theological premise in the religious publishing industry that the foundation for stewardship is avoiding debt. But I wonder about that.

The last home I built for my wife and I was actually an old wooden barn. Don't ask me why, but I've always wanted to convert an old barn into a house. In 1998 we bought an old barn, and I began renovating it into our home. It's a great building to live in, with hand-hewn oak beams everywhere and lots of open space. But to hook the house up to the septic system, I had to dig a trench through a concrete floor! So I rented a jackhammer from a tool-rental company and went at it.

Now that jackhammer was pretty expensive by the hour. In fact, if I had used it for a week, I could have bought one cheaper than renting one. But I only needed the jackhammer for a couple of hours, so I rented it. Carrying debt is the same thing: renting something you don't need to own. If you want to buy a car to get you to work, you don't need to own all the money it takes to buy the car (the capital), you can rent that money for just the time you need it. And with a simple interest loan, you can pay both the rent (the interest) and some of the money (the principle) each month. The same thing is true for a mortgage on a house. You don't need to own all the money it takes to buy a house; you can rent some of it, and pay it back a little at a time while at the same time paying rent (interest) on what you were using the previous month. So not all debt is bad.

There's smart debt and there's not-so-smart debt. Smart debt is debt on the money it takes to make money, or debt on something that appreciates in value. A house, for example, usually increases in value over the years, depending on the local housing market, the location, and the general economic situation. And you can live in it at the same time! Remember, you can't live in a mutual fund!

One way to think about a mortgage is to consider the interest portion of your payment as the rent you would pay if you were just leasing the house instead of buying it. Consider the portion that goes toward the principle as savings. If the value of your house rises, then the difference between what it used to be worth and what it's now worth is also a form of savings. What more could you want, a place to live and two forms of savings—all from one mortgage!

Likewise, going into debt to buy a car to get to work is smart debt. That debt will make it possible to create the income to pay the rent on the borrowed money, and more. Of course, the goal would be to borrow the money for the next car from yourself instead of from the bank again. And that leads us to what I call my "debt to savings conversion plan."

One of the easiest ways to begin saving for retirement is to just keep making those payments to yourself once that loan is paid off—and invest the savings! This, of course, means that you'll have to choose to not trade in your car for a newer one before the loan is paid off, and that you'll be spending a little more on car repair and maintenance. But experience has shown that Americans buy cars for emotional reasons rather than mechanical ones, and that it's almost always cheaper to repair a vehicle than to replace it. If you keep making those payments to yourself after your loan is paid off, when it comes time to replace that older car you'll have a large savings account to borrow from. By the way, you'll probably be much nicer—and cheaper—to borrow from than any bank!

The following exercise will show just how much your present loan payment is worth for your future retirement if you're 47.5 years old and have a car payment of $350 per month on a used car you just bought on a 30 month loan contract:

Step 1: Evaluate your current situation

a. How much is your car/consumer loan payment? $350 per month

b. When will that loan be paid off? 2.5 years from now

c. When do you want to be financially independent? 17.5 years from now

d. How many years are there between your loan payoff and your financial independence time goal? 15 years

Step 2: Determine expected return rate

Decide the rate of return by which you want your savings to grow. If you're 35 years old or younger when you begin to save for financial independence, you can afford to be fairly aggressive. Higher growth rates demand higher risk, but investments have historically returned the following rates:

a. aggressive growth (mostly common stocks) 12 percent

b. balanced growth & income (stocks and bonds) 9 percent

c. safety and conservation (mostly bonds & CDs) 6 percent

Step 3: Calculate savings

Now find the appropriate compound factor from the chart below and multiply your payment amount by that factor to find the total saved if you just keep making that loan payment and invest the savings in the appropriate investment class.

	12% return	9% return	6% return
2 years	26.9	26.2	25.4
4 years	61.2	57.5	54.1
6 years	105	95	86.5
8 years	160	140	123
10 years	230	194	164
15 years	500	378	291
20 years	989	668	462
25 years	2085	1218	739
30 years	3495	1831	1005

500 X $ 350 per month = $ 175,000

Hey, no problem saving what I need for financial independence—all I need to do is buy a car and keep it! Isn't it amazing what a car payment amounts to over time? If you buy your car when you're 25 and save that same car payment for the next 30 years, your savings will total over one million dollars, even accounting for the cars you'll buy from your own savings in the interim. Who would have thought that debt could be so useful?

Study Questions

1. Have you ever paid off a loan? What did the extra money in your pocket feel like that first month? How long was it before there wasn't any "extra" money?

2. If you did the exercise in this chapter, what was the grand total of savings that your loan payment would be worth if you just kept making payments?

3. Did this exercise change how you feel about debt?

4. List your debts, and next to each one put a plus sign (+) if you consider it to be a "smart" debt, and a minus sign (-) if you consider it to be a "not-so-smart" debt. Now, think about how you might pay off the ones with the minus signs next to them as soon as you can.

11

Chapter Eleven

You Can't Live In A Mutual Fund!

I used to be a builder. Not a very successful one, I'll admit. I've built only 12 houses in my life so far, and three of those have been for myself. But I like houses. I especially liked designing the homes I built for myself. There's something about putting your own personality into the design of the house you live in. I love the home I built out of that old barn. Don't ask me why: it's hard to heat; with a wind outside you can fly a kite in my bedroom; and the groundhogs and raccoons who lived there before still want the place back! But it's my barn, and what I did on the inside is an extension of my personality.

Building is a challenge to me. For example, to span the six feet from the landing at the top of the stairs to the beginning of the floor in my wife's office on the seventh level of the barn, I built a swinging bridge. I'm not a "swinger," nor do I live a particularly "swinging" life. But anyone can build a solid bridge. And overcoming the challenge of getting from one place to another in an interesting way delights me.

The same might be said for building your life to be a "display of the surpassing riches of God's kindness toward us in Christ Jesus." That's a challenge, but one with interesting possibilities. For example, the typical advice to those starting on their career paths is to get started on retirement savings as soon as possible. Companies have a variety of savings plans available: 401Ks, direct deposit savings, discount stock purchases, etc. The problem is that you can't live in a mutual fund (401K, savings account, stock certificate)!

Home ownership is a good alternative for building savings for financial independence almost everywhere in North America. In only a few urban areas do the current costs of purchasing a home and the inherent risks of the location seem to dictate against buying. For example, in the earthquake zone of southern California the housing market is priced at perhaps the highest cost per square foot anywhere in the U.S., but the next earthquake will severely lower the value of all the homes in the area. In such a situation a renter has none of the risks of a lowered valuation, nor any of the insurance or tax consequences.

In most areas of North America, the only serious financial question about buying a home is, "How much is enough house?" And that depends on what your house means to you. At the very least a house means home, a place to live and raise a family. A house can also mean investment, a place to put money to create a return in future years.

What about other stuff? Like food. Ok, I'll admit it. I'm a little overweight. For some reason I tend to gain weight in the fall and winter and lose in the spring and summer. It isn't some internal calendar that drives this cycle; it's just that the more time I spend in the house, the more I eat. And the more time I spend working outside, the less I eat. As I write this at the end of winter, I'm about six pounds heavier than I was six months ago. I'd like to lose the six pounds I've gained since last September.

If you want to get really overwhelmed by different opinions on how to lose weight, do a search on the internet using the word "diet," like I did recently. It seemed like a million sites came up. And half of them were selling a magic pill of one kind or another. "Lose weight while you sleep!" was the promise in the ads on those web sites. The other half of the sites promote one diet or another, all of which are based on deprivation and avoidance.

However, if you want to see some helpful stuff on the internet about losing weight, do a similar search (on the internet or in the library) using the word "overeating" instead of "diet." There are still a lot of sites, but not nearly as many. One of the most helpful I've found is sponsored by Carol Solomon, a counselor based in Chicago who has a web site that promotes her on-line book titled Lose Weight and Keep It Off! (www.lose-weight-now-stay-slim-forever). She provides what I've been looking for: a way to keep from regaining the weight I lose each spring.

Ms. Solomon says that one of the problems behind overeating is that most Americans don't know how to recognize the physical feeling of having enough. At least in my case she's dead right! I don't know what it feels like to be full, much less what it feels like to be hungry. When I'm home I eat three times a day, because that's when there's food on the table. My wife is a great cook, and I'm not going to miss any meal she cooks. She prepares a marinated leg of lamb for Easter that grown men have been known to burst into tears over—just from the pure joy of eating it! And the three-layer cheesecake that she makes on my birthday is so good that if they don't have that in heaven, I'm considering not going! (Just kidding!) But the point is, it's not because I'm hungry that I eat; I eat because I love my wife's cooking.

Now here's the weird part. When I'm travelling, I still eat three times a day! Not because it's great food (Have you tried what they serve as airline food these days?). I eat in airport and freeway restaurants because it's time to eat. Why do I do that? With very few exceptions, the food choices available to travelers are over-priced, over-rated, and over-caloried. No one goes to an airport to eat out! Carol Solomon points out in her book that we can avoid over-eating by first knowing why we're eating, and then by paying attention to the physical sensations that tell us when we've had enough.

I used to be "overweight" when it came to the cars I bought as well. Like loving to eat and hating being overweight, I used to both love and hate buying cars. I love going around "kicking tires." I like the smell of a new car, even if it comes out of a spray can that only dealers can buy. And I even like bargaining with the salesman. But I also hate trying to decide which individual car I want. And I hate the thought that comes after buying: if I'd been a better bargainer, I could have saved some money. I really hate the thought that while driving away in the car I finally bought, the salesman was gleefully telling his buddies what a sucker I was.

But now that I know (from chapter 6) that the inherent usefulness of a car is reliable transportation, and not a physical attempt to be more loved or seem more important, I really love buying cars. And that's because I buy cars in a very different way than I ever did before.

The first thing I do when I think I need to replace a car is to decide why I want to do it in the first place. And since reliable transportation is the meaning I've decided to attach to a car, I measure both the reliability and the transportation that I am getting out of the car I now own. For example, my last car was a great car. It was just the right size for my calling (getting to the airport on time), it got great gas mileage, and it even was fun to drive. It was good transportation.

However, it was starting to sputter a bit now and then, and it did have 279,000 miles on it. I can replace some things on a car like broken belts, old spark plugs, and ignition wires. But that's not something I want or can afford to do on the way to the airport. The reliability of my twelve-year-old car had dipped below my requirements. And that meant that it was time to replace it with something more reliable.

The next step was to decide what make and model I should buy. This step is almost a much fun as kicking tires. In fact it's a lot like kicking tires, except you do it at the library or in front of your computer. The first thing to do is find some way of evaluating reliability, and that's the easy part. All you have to do is to do a search among magazines or online for reliability surveys. Consumers Reports has an annual auto issue that evaluates all the new cars for that year. If you turn to the back of the magazine you'll also find their listing of the best and worst used cars in terms of most reliable and most troublesome. In that listing I found that my current car, a Geo Prism, ranks right up there in the list of most reliable with the Ford Escort, the Honda Acura and Civic, the complete Toyota line, and a number of other vehicles.

If you have access to the internet (something you can usually find at the library), one of the best sources online is at http://www.autooninfo.net. At that web site, like—Consumer Reports—they have a listing of the best and worst of any particular year. For example, for the year 1994 the Mazda MX-5 Miata ranked most reliable, with a rating of +1.00, and the Toyota and Honda sedans followed close behind. The Chevy S-10 Blazer and the Dodge Intrepid were at the bottom.

This helps me know what I should look for: something like my Geo Prism, a Toyota Corolla, a Honda Civic, or a Ford Escort. But I hate trying to figure out which particular car I like, and I don't like trying to outwit the salesman to get a fair price on a particular car. However, if reliable transportation is the goal and if I already have a good idea what kind of car will be reliable, all I have to do now is to figure out what transportation is worth to me.

Since the miles I'll get out of the car in the future—and not the color or model or what someone else will pay for it—determine its value to me, then I should be able to calculate value by dividing what I paid for my last car by the number of miles I got out of it. I paid $6,250 for my last Geo Prism (actually a Toyota Corolla with a Chevy body on it), and I drove it trouble free for 200,000 miles after I bought it. If you divide 6250 by 200,000, you get 3.125 cents per mile. That was ten years ago, and I can't expect to pay the same now as I did then, so I need to calculate the difference caused by inflation. According to the U.S. government, inflation on automobiles has averaged about 4.5% over the last ten years. At an annual inflation rate of 4.5%, 3.125 cents becomes 4. 875 cents, so I rounded my value figure off to 5 cents per mile.

I called two used car dealers and told them that I was looking for a replacement for my Geo Prism, "something in the Toyota Corolla/Honda Civic/Ford Escort line." I also mentioned that since I was just looking for reliable transportation, I didn't care what color it was, how old it was, or how many miles were on it. I told them that according to my calculations, that kind of car was worth something less than 5 cents per "future mile."

Both dealers said exactly the same thing when they heard that term, "future mile": "Huh?" I explained that the only value a car has for me has to do with the future miles I could get out of it. The way to calculate that was to subtract the miles on the car from 200,000 (the number of miles I think one of these cars should go without major repairs). I then reiterated that I would be willing to pay up to 5 cents per mile for whatever that number of miles was. Two months later (you can't be in a hurry) I got a phone call from one of the dealers telling me he had a car that might fit what I had asked for. It was another Geo Prism, with 80,000 miles on it, and they wanted $5995.

If you follow my calculations, that car was worth 120,000 x $.05, which is $6,000, so it was in my price range. I drove the car to see if I could detect any problems while it was in motion, and then I checked out the engine by listening for any unusual sounds. (A more cautious approach might be to pay a mechanic to check it out for you.) Satisfied, I told the salesman that I was willing to pay $6000 for the car, and asked him if they didn't want the extra five dollars. To my surprise, he replied that there was a $1000 off" sale that weekend, and that I could have the car for $4995! "Ok," I said, "but I'm willing to pay $6000." "No," he replied, "$4995 is the price." That's the kind of bargaining I like!

What this car salesman taught me was that if he could afford to sell that car for $4995, the inflation rate for used cars is more like 3% than 4.5%. I bought that car for a projected 4.25 cents per future mile. Every time I buy a car I learn something, but this time it was something worth $1000!

Study Questions

1. How much per mile did it cost you to own your last car? (Hint: subtract what you got in trade in value or what you sold the car for from what you paid for it. Then divide that amount by the number of miles you put on the car while you owned it.)

2. Go "tire-kicking" and see if you could buy another car of approximately the same size and style from a used car dealer for the same price per future mile. (Hint: subtract the mileage on the car from 200,000 and multiply that number by the answer to question 1.)

3. Pick out a car you like, calculate what it's worth by the "per future mile" method, and tell the car dealer that this is only hypothetical, but if you were in the market, that amount is what you would be willing to pay for that car. How did he or she react? How did you feel in that discussion? Was it a different feeling that you had from the last time you bought a car?

12

Chapter Twelve

Never Think About the Gold

In the Eastern Orthodox tradition, certain monks are described as "God's Holy Fools." These religious people intentionally hide their spirituality and biblical knowledge behind a façade of foolishness. In the 19th century one of the most well-known Holy Fools was a monk name Feofil, of the Kiev-Caves Monastery. Although he was inwardly a highly devout person, in his commitment to humility he hid his devotion behind a pattern of bizarre behavior. No one understood him. No one, that is, except those simple folk who came to him for blessing and advice. They were the ones whose souls benefited.

Every once in a while today I meet some who fits the description of God's Holy Fool. These are people who if they weren't among friends would likely be locked up. In any other setting they would be certifiably crazy. One of the craziest people I know is a pastor by the name of Ricky Regier

He not only fits the description of being one of God's Holy Fools, he is also one of the most contented people I know. When I met Ricky in Hubbard, Oregon, in 1993, he knew he was in the right place at the right time doing the right thing. He was contented with absolutely everything. And one Sunday afternoon he taught me something about contentment that I've never forgotten.

That morning I'd presented part of a seminar I was doing at the Zion Mennonite church in Hubbard. During the worship service we'd had a wonderful experience of the presence of God, and we went from that amazing moment to a wonderful Sunday dinner that filled up whatever empty spaces were left in our bodies and souls. And then, because Ricky had something he wanted to show me, we went for a walk.

What Ricky wanted to show me was a steel sailboat that a neighbor was building down the road. What a boat! I build boats as a hobby, but in my wildest dreams I've never contemplated building anything this grand. After looking it over we headed down the road for home to take a nap before the evening's activities. Just as we turned the corner for Ricky's home, the sun came out from behind the clouds. According to Ricky, Oregon doesn't have many sunny days, so this was as close to a miracle as they get around there. And as if that wasn't enough, there in front of us stood Mount Hood, covered with snow that reflected the sun from behind us.

Ricky turned to me and with a big smile on his face, said, "You know, this is good enough! There doesn't have to be a heaven. This is good enough!" Not only was he right, but he had just put into words what I'd been thinking. Boy, was he right. At that moment life was as good as it gets—so good that we both would've been happy to die right then. We were content. Ever since then, when things are going really well, I find myself thinking, "Take me now Lord, it can't get any better than this." That's what I identify as ultimate contentment.

However, are we supposed to be content in spiritual matters? Aren't we supposed to have a "holy hunger" for God and for what God has for us? Didn't Jesus himself tell us to "Ask and it shall be given to you," and "Seek first the Kingdom of God"? Of course he did; God has more for us than what we have right now. Where, then, is the place of contentment in spirituality?

How to get more from God is a hot topic. Bookstores are full of little books that claim to have the secret to getting God to give you what you want. The problem is that focusing on getting more from God is not how God wants us to spend our time. A statement of common wisdom says, "You can't have your cake and eat it too." That seems obvious; if you eat your cake, you no longer have it. Contentment and wanting more of God, however, can exist together. When it comes to your relationship with God, you can have your cake and eat it too! You can be contented and still seek more of God. In fact, here's another secret I can't keep to my self: "With contentment comes blessing."

The scriptures are full of statements describing how God wants us to spend our time. God wants us to "be a certain kind of Firstfruits among His creatures" (James 1:18); God wants us to "display the surpassing riches of His kindness toward us in Christ Jesus (Ephesians 2:7); and Paul says, "For we are His workmanship, created in Christ Jesus for good works, which God prepared beforehand, that we would walk in them" (Ephesians 2:10). Wow! God has a plan for us, and it has nothing to do with our figuring out how to get more from God.

In His salvation God has given us everything we need to "live saved." His Son redeemed us from our independence; He resurrected His Son to redeem us from death; and His

Spirit lives within us so that whatever we go through in life we'll not go through it alone. God did all of that for a reason: so that we will be a redeeming offering to someone sometime. Nowhere in scripture does it say that God saved us so that we can spend the rest of our lives begging Him for more and more blessings, and then finally when we have it all, we can go to heaven when we die. That might be the American Dream version of the good news, but it's not the Gospel of Jesus Christ found in the Bible.

The Gospel of Jesus Christ is the message that we've been set free in God's stewardship to be a gift of God to the rest of His world. First you have to know for sure that God loves you. If you have any doubt about that, you'll always be thinking about how to keep God happy. Believe it or not, doing something to make God happy is a biblical idea. The Greek word for that is propitiate—to make happy. Making God happy isn't just a Christian idea, by the way. Hindus spend most of their spiritual energy trying to make their gods happy. In fact, a friend of mine who used to be a Hindu told me that the whole purpose of being a Hindu was to keep the gods—especially Kali, the goddess of destruction—from getting mad at you.

In the gospel however, God is "made happy" not by something we do, but by something God did. John says that "He loved us and sent His son to be a propitiation for our sins" (1 John 4:10). John also says that if God did that for us, then we should do that for one another; we should love one another. In the gospel of Jesus Christ, God always acts first. God makes the first move and then asks us to follow it, to do it in return. But God also "always bats last," as a friend of mine says. We don't have to worry about the future, for we know that God wins. We can keep our minds on the task at hand, for God has the future in His hand.

It's like the story of the village where there was a famously generous man. Any time anyone needed something—help, food, money, no matter what it was—this man was ready to give. The funny thing was that this man had no job, no bank account, no visible source of the wealth he was distributing so generously. He just seemed to have an inexhaustible supply of small gold pieces.

In this same village lived a discontented young man who had noticed the man's apparent wealth and had begun watching the generous man closely. He noticed that every once in a while the man would disappear into his house and not reappear for two or three days. Once when the man had disappeared into his house, the young man put a stepladder up to the house and began looking into the windows. After several tries, he found the window that looked into the room where the man had disappeared. He saw the man sitting on a small stool in front of a large cast-iron pot. He watched as the man poured dirt into the pot from a bucket, added water from a pitcher, and begin stirring the pot with a wooden spoon. That's all he did—just sat there and stirred that pot.

When he finally stopped stirring, he reached into the pot with his bare hand and felt around for a moment. When he drew his hand out, in it was a small piece of pure gold. The man took the piece of gold and put it into a small wooden bowl with many other pieces of gold.

Aha! the young man watching all this thought, that's how he does it! Just then the ladder slipped and the young man fell to the ground with a loud clatter. Before he could jump up and run away, the man from the house was standing over him.

"What were you doing?" asked the older man, "Spying on me?"

"Yes," admitted the embarrassed younger man, "I wanted to know how you got all that money you give away, and now I know."

"Well, if you had asked me, I would have told you," the man said. "It's not a secret. You just put some dirt in the pot, and then some water, and then you stir it until the piece of gold appears."

Before the older man could say anything else, the young man jumped up and ran home. He found a cast iron pot, dug up some dirt from his garden, drew some water from the well, poured the two things into the pot, and began stirring the mix with a wooden spoon. After a while he reached into the pot and felt around, but there was nothing there except mud—no gold pieces. So he began stirring again—he stirred and stirred—and again he reached into the pot and felt around. But again there was nothing in the pot except mud. He did this several more times, each time without success, each time with more and more frustration. Finally he stomped out of his house, went to the home of the older man, and banged loudly on the door.

The door opened and before the older man could say anything, the younger man grabbed him by the shirt and yelled, "You lied to me! I did what you said and no matter how long I stirred I didn't get any gold!"

"I didn't lie to you, replied the older man. You ran off before I could tell you the most important thing."

"What is it?" demanded the younger man. "Tell me!"

"The most important thing is that when you're stirring the pot, you must think only of the poor who need your help; you must never think of the gold."

People who are always thinking of the rewards of faith will never be content in the life they have. But people who are always thinking of the journey of faith will never be dissatisfied with what life brings. Yes, it is possible to be content and have a holy hunger. Our desire for more of God is found in ministering to those God sends our way, not in the "stirring of the pot." We find spiritual contentment in our following of Jesus, not in our thinking or praying or begging for more blessings.

Study Questions

1. Have you ever felt that "it can't get any better than this"? What was the occasion? Where were you, and how do you describe the feeling?

2. What do you want to know more about in terms of your spiritual life? Where do you want to grow?

3. Is there a peace in your hunger to know God more? Will it be okay with you if you die without knowing more?

13

Chapter Thirteen

Good News and Bad News

My favorite good news/bad news joke is about the fellow who had a bunch of medical tests and a week later went to see his physician to hear the results.

The doctor said to him, "Well, I have good news and bad news. Which do you want first?"

The fellow gulped a few times, and finally said, "What's the good news?"

"You have three days to live," said the doctor.

"Good grief!" gasped the man, "If that's the good news, what's the bad news?"

"The bad news is that I was supposed to tell you that two days ago!"

Well, now that you're almost to the end of this book, I'm afraid I have some good news and some bad news for you. The good news is that learning contentment can change your life in a way that almost nothing else can. Having the power of "enough" will set you free from the consumer-driven search for love and status, and you'll now have the ability to model God's extravagant entrepreneurial steward-ship to a world that is still looking for more.

But now for the bad news! Just reading about something seldom results in the changes one wants to make, and you must be interested in changing or you wouldn't have bought this book in the first place! To see any real changes happen in our lives, we must apply the good ideas we learn about to our behavior. It's sort of like what Jesus said to the lawyer at the end of the Good Samaritan story, "Go thou, and do like-wise!"

This book was not written just to present another good idea; it was written to help you make a drastic change in your relationship with stuff. You can't get away from stuff—in fact you shouldn't get away from stuff. But stuff needs to be put in its place. A good way to start changing your relationship with stuff is to work through the exercises that follow:

What Stuff Means?

1. Following each word in the list below, write down what that thing means to you at the moment, or what it meant before you read this book. There are no wrong answers.
   - House
   - Car
   - Salary
   - Food
   - Clothes
   - Cash Savings
   - Retirement Savings

2. Now reflect on how you formed those opinions. Think of what your parents taught you about stuff. What were the

unspoken lessons you learned about possessions? Were you aware of your family being rich or poor? How did your family handle money? Write your thoughts below.

3. Now go back to question 1 and ask yourself which of your beliefs about stuff are working for you and which are working against you. Cross out the ones that seem to detract from your life, and circle the ones that seem to still make sense. Consider reflecting on the content of Chapter 5 to help you think through your feelings toward stuff.

4. Since you learned what stuff means from somewhere, you're free to change your mind about what stuff means. Take a look again at Chapter 6 and try to determine the inherent usefulness that each category of your stuff has in your life.

5. Now that you've determined the inherent usefulness of your stuff, you can calculate when you have enough. For example, if your house means "hospitality," ask yourself how much house you need to be hospitable. Do you need an extra bedroom, or is there a room now used to store stuff that could be used to house someone who needs a bed for the night? Do you need to get more towels and bedding to be hospitable? Look at each word below, and write down what is enough in relation to that item.

- House

- Car

- Salary

- Food

- Clothes

- Cash Savings
- Retirement Savings (see chapter 9 or worksheet below)

Retirement savings worksheet

The following assumes that future growth and interest rates will be similar to historical rates, and that inflation rates for simple-living Christians are less than those for people living the typical secular lifestyle.

Step 1.
Decide how much you want to pay yourself when you "retire.'

$_____ /month x 12 = $_____ /year needed retirement income

Step 2.
Pick the rate of return (after taxes) you think your capital will provide during those years. (Higher returns demand higher risk, but fairly safe returns can reasonably be expected to be from 5 to 8 percent.) Now divide your yearly retirement income needs by that rate (in hundredths).

$_____ /0.0 = $_____Total capital needed in today's dollars

Step 3.
a. When do you want to start paying yourself? _____ years old

b. Write down your current age. _____ years old

c. Subtract b. from a. to get "years until retirement" _____ years

Step 4.
Now find your "inflation factor" fromt the following table (the percent "simple living rate") and multiply "total capital" by it to find your "retirement capital."

Years

2	4	6	8	10	12	14
1.04	1.08	1.13	1.17	1.22	1.27	1.32

16	18	20	25	30	35	40
1.37	1.43	1.49	1.64	1.81	2.0	2.21

$_____X_____ Inflation factor = $_____Retirement dollars

Step 5.
Pick the rate of growth you project for your capital if invested now:
10 percent — aggresive growth (mostly commom stocks)
7.5 percent — balanced growth and income (stocks and bonds)
5 percent — safety and conversation (mostly bonds and CDs)

Step 6.
From the following chart, find the multiplier for your combination of "years to retirement" and "projected growth rate."

Years

	2	4	6	8	10	12	14	16	18	20	25	30
10%	.8264	.6830	.5465	.4665	.3855	.3186	.2633	.2176	.1799	.1486	.0923	.0573
7.5%	.8653	.7488	.507	.4852	.4852	.4199	.3633	.3144	.2720	.2354	.1640	.1142
5%	.9070	.8227	.7462	.6768	.6139	.5568	.5051	.4581	.4155	.3769	.2953	.2314

Step 7.
Multiply this factor times "retirement capital needed" (Step 4) to get "retirement savings needed now."

_____ X $ _____ = $_____

Step 8.
Does this equal your actual retirement savings? Are you "in the ballpark?"

Yes? Congratulations, you are now free to give away your life! If your growth rate and inflation assumptions remain accurate, from now until the day you "retire," you may be able to work for only room and board and health care.

No? you can get there by:

1. Increasing the growth rate in Step 5 by making higher risk investments;
2. Increasing your rate of savings for retirement; or
3. Adjusting your desired "retirement income" to meet financial realities.

So, what did you find? Do you have enough? Are there areas of your material life where you found that you actually didn't have enough of something, at least yet? And if, for example, you found that you didn't have enough retirement savings so that when you want to be financially independent you will be able to pay yourself what you need, when will you reach that point? And if you found that you were already at the point of being able to say, "I'm there, and from now on I can afford to put my excess time and money into other ventures", have you thought about what those "other ventures" might be? What, in other words, is your **passion**? What is it that you would do if you had the time and freedom to do so? What sets your imagination on fire when you think of where you would really like to give away the rest of your life?

That after all is really what this book is about, learning to achieve contentment so that you can focus on your passion rather than your need for "stuff". The apostle James says that we have been "called forth to be His Firstfruits to the rest of His creation". (James 1:18) That means that God has something in mind for us other than a "comfortable retirement at the end of the American Dream". And what God has in mind is going to be different for each of us, a "calling" specific to our interests, skills, and talents, so there isn't going to be a next chapter titled "Where God Wants You To Go," or "What God Wants You To Do". I can't tell you what God has in mind for you. But God can tell you that.

And that is the last thing I want you to do. No more worksheets, no more exercises or study questions, just an encouragement to seek the will of God for the rest of your life. And that's not hard to do at all. Just ask, and then just listen, and then just say "Yes"! In fact, that is a pretty good rule to follow to find God's will at any stage of life: Ask, Listen, and Say **Yes!** And God will bless you as you go in the contentment you find by living in His presence.

Lynn Miller